The Gold Badge

Written by Karen King
Illustrated by Vanessa Henson

PYRFORD PRIMARY SCHOOL
COLDHARBOUR ROAD
PYRFORD, WOKING
SURREY GU22 8SP

Collins Educational
An Imprint of HarperCollins*Publishers*

Chapter One

Jack crossed his fingers and stared at Mr Briggs, the head teacher. Mr Briggs was just about to announce the winner of the gold badge in Class 2. Jack hoped it was him.

"Now for Class 2," said Mr Briggs. He looked at the children sitting on the hall floor. Class 2 were right in front, all waiting eagerly for his next words.

"This week the gold badge has been awarded to Sophie Jenkins for neat handwriting."

Everyone clapped as Sophie stood up and walked over to claim the badge. Neat handwriting, Jack sighed, no wonder he hadn't won the badge.

Last week Dalwar had won the badge for maths so Jack had been working hard on his maths all week. But he hadn't made very much progress. The week before Ben had won it for painting. Jack was hopeless at painting.

A gold badge was awarded to someone in each class every Monday.

The child wore the badge proudly all week then handed it back on Friday for it to be awarded to someone else. Jack had been at Riddington Junior School for two months, but he had never won the badge. He was beginning to think he never would.

"I've won the Gold Badge twice," Emily told him.

Jack turned and stared at her in surprise. Emily wasn't very clever, her handwriting was awful and the only thing she could paint were matchstick men. How did she win the gold badge?

"What did you win it for?" asked Jack.

"Being helpful. And having a nice smile," replied Emily.

"I thought you only got the badge for good work," said Jack.

Emily shook her head, "No, you can win it for anything. I won it for helping people and smiling."

Well, I can do that, Jack thought. Next week he was going to win the gold badge. He'd make sure of it.

Chapter Two

The next morning Jack walked into the classroom with a big smile on his face.

"What are you grinning at?" asked Simon. He touched his newly-cut hair and glared at Jack.

"Nothing," said Jack, smiling.

"Better not be," muttered Simon under his breath.

Jack just kept smiling.

Jack smiled all week.

He smiled when Mrs Tipton told him
he'd got all his sums wrong on

Tuesday. He smiled
when Mrs Tipton
told the class off
for being noisy
on Wednesday.
He smiled when
Mrs Tipton drew a red line through
his handwriting on Thursday and told

him to do it all
over again. And
he smiled when
he tripped up and
dropped the red
paint all over the
floor on Friday.

"I don't know what's the matter with you this week, Jack. You've been acting very strangely," Mrs Tipton said crossly. "And I wish you would take that silly grin off your face. It isn't funny to spill paint."

Jack stopped smiling. He had an awful feeling that he wasn't going to win the gold badge on Monday.

He was right. Simon got it for putting his things away tidily.

Jack decided that he would try to win the badge by being helpful.

He sneaked into the classroom early next morning and looked around for something to do to help Mrs Tipton. Then he noticed that the wall frieze had fallen down. Mrs Tipton would be really pleased if he stuck it back up, Jack thought.

It took ages to stick the frieze back on the wall. As soon as he got one side to stick, the other side fell down again.

He had just finished when the other children and Mrs Tipton came into the classroom.

"Jack! What on earth are you doing?" asked Mrs Tipton. "You know you aren't supposed to be in here until the bell."

"Please, miss, the wall frieze fell down so I stuck it back up again," Jack told her.

Mrs Tipton wasn't very pleased.

"It didn't fall down. I took it down so I could put up some paintings," she said. "So take it down again, please."

Jack looked for other ways to help.

Next day Jack volunteered to take the register to the office for Mrs Tipton. He wanted to please her by being quick, so he ran along the corridor. But as he turned the corner he crashed into Mr Weston.

Mr Weston dropped the pile of papers he was carrying all over the floor.

"Sorry, sir," said Jack, scooping the papers up quickly.

"You know that it's against the school rules to run along the corridors, Jack," said Mr Weston. "These papers are for Mrs Tipton and now they're all screwed up and dirty. She won't be very pleased with you."

Mrs Tipton wasn't pleased. She was very cross.

Jack was beginning to think he wouldn't win the gold badge for helping, after all.

He was right. On Monday, Sara won the badge for writing a poem.

Chapter Three

The next day Mrs Tipton told them they were going to make models from junk.

"I want you all to make a model of any kind of transport," she told them. "It can be a plane, a car, a train, a spaceship or an idea of your own. You must make it out of junk like tubes, cardboard boxes and yoghurt pots."

Jack was excited. He was good at making models. Now he had a good chance of winning the gold badge.

Mrs Tipton gave the children a piece of paper each, and said, "Draw a picture of your model. Then write down the things you will need to make it. Remember, it must be all your own work."

Jack did a brilliant picture of a spaceship. Then he wrote a list of the things he would need: tubes, sticky tape, glue. Dad helped him spell some of the words.

"I'm going to make the best model ever then I'll win the gold badge," he told Dad.

"Good for you," said Dad.

Jack worked hard on his model all week.

On Friday morning he took his model into school. Everyone else took their models, too. When Jack saw all the other spaceships he knew he wasn't going to win the gold badge.

He was right. On Monday, Ramona won the badge for her model bus.

"I'm never going to win the gold badge," Jack told Dad that evening as he got into bed.

"Of course you will," said Dad. "You just have to keep trying."

"I've tried," Jack told him miserably. "I've tried doing good work but someone is always cleverer than me. I've tried smiling and being helpful but it always goes wrong. And I've tried making the best model ever but that didn't work either."

"Then you'll have to try something else," said Dad. "Don't worry, you'll get the badge one week, you'll see."

Jack lay awake thinking about it for a while. In the end he drifted off to sleep and dreamed that he had won the gold badge for being the cleverest boy in the school.

Chapter Four

The next day a new boy joined their class.

"This is Gregory Davies," said Mrs Tipton. "His parents have just moved house so Gregory is joining our school. Now I want you all to make him welcome."

Jack looked at Gregory. He looked very nervous, just how Jack felt on his first day.

Mrs Tipton told Gregory to sit by Anna. Then she started to tell the class about their new project.

"It must be something to do with summer," she said. "So you can write about your holidays, the plants and animals we see in summer or even write a poem about summer. You must work in pairs and the project has to be finished by next Friday."

Jack sighed. He wasn't very good at projects.

"Now I want you all to choose your partners," Mrs Tipton said. "Wait until I call your names out then tell me who you would like your partner to be."

One by one the children chose their best friends.

Jack was trying to decide between Christopher and Dalwar, who were sort of his best friends. But then he noticed that Gregory was looking miserably down at his desk.

"He's scared to look up because he knows no one will choose him," thought Jack. And he remembered how awful he had felt when he was new to the school.

"I'd like Gregory to be my partner," he said.

Mrs Tipton beamed and Gregory went bright red. "That's very nice of you, Jack," she said.

Gregory and Jack sat together so they could work on their project.

"What shall we do the project about?" asked Jack. Gregory frowned. "Er… summer holidays?" he suggested.

Jack agreed that this sounded easy, so they started work.

Chapter Five

Jack and Gregory worked really hard on their project. They cut out pictures from travel brochures and glued them in their project book. They wrote about the places they had been on holiday.

"It's a good project," Jack said when they'd finished. "We might even win the gold badge."

"What's that?" asked Gregory. Jack explained.

"But how can we share a badge?" asked Gregory.

Jack thought. "Well, I'll wear it until Wednesday lunch time and you can wear it for the rest of the week," he said.

When they took their project into school on Friday, Jack knew they weren't going to win. Nearly all the class had done a project on summer holidays except Christopher and Dalwar who had written about butterflies.

"Sorry. It was a silly idea to write about summer holidays," said Gregory. "You should have chosen one of your friends instead."

Jack shrugged. "It doesn't matter. Anyway, you're my friend too, aren't you?"

Gregory grinned.

The next Monday, Jack tried not to listen while Mr Briggs announced the winner of the gold badge. But he couldn't help it. His ears were straining as he tried to hear.

"This week's winner of the gold badge in Class 2 is Jack Williams," said Mr Briggs.

Jack was so astonished his mouth dropped open. What had he done?

Mr Briggs smiled over at Jack.

"Last week a new boy, Gregory Davies, joined Class 2. Jack has been so kind and helpful to him that Mrs Tipton has awarded him the gold badge. Well done, Jack!"

Jack could hardly believe it. He'd actually won the gold badge. Almost in a dream he got to his feet and walked over to Mr Briggs.

Almost in a dream he heard everyone clap as Mr Briggs pinned the badge to his jumper. And almost in a dream he went back to join the rest of the class. He sat down and felt the badge. It was real all right. A big grin spread over his face. Wait until he showed Dad.

Gregory nudged him. "Do you think I'll ever win the gold badge?" he whispered.

"Sure you will," Jack told him. "You just have to keep trying. Then one day you'll win it too."